A Congress WBN Publication

Produced By:

 and

DISCOVERING God TOGETHER

Discovery Workbook #2

THIS BOOK BELONGS TO:
_____

About the WE MAGNIFY YOU Discovery Workbook Series

Our families are at the core of our Kingdom Communities. The WE MAGNIFY YOU album provides us with a wonderful opportunity to develop and strengthen the expression of worship in our homes.

Each We Magnify You Discovery Workbook has been designed for parents, guardians, teachers and children to experience and explore the songs together.

Discover new sight of what it means to magnify, exalt and praise our God. Together, our families will develop a deeper and stronger understanding of who God is, releasing a whole-hearted expression of worship unto Him.

For each song on the WE MAGNIFY YOU album, we have a Workbook with the lyrics and specially created activities.

Enjoy taking time together to consider what the lyrics mean. Explore scripture verses that tell us more about each song. Engage in fun activities, including word puzzles and coloring games.

Through it all we can together gain a deeper understanding of how the words we sing reflect the lives we must live, as we align ourselves to God.

Now that is a beautiful thing!

Guidance for Parents

The WE MAGNIFY YOU worship album from Congress MusicFactory contains prayers and songs from Dr. Woodroffe and saints from Elijah Centre and Kingdom Communities across Congress WBN.

WE MAGNIFY YOU is a powerful expression of worship and praise to our Lord. Each workbook in the We Magnify You Discovery Series explores the lyrics of the songs, sharing explanations, key scriptures and fun activities.

These resources will help us to align our lives, our families and our communities to the words that we lift unto God.

UNTO YOU

LYRICS

We lift our eyes
Unto You
We lift our hands
Unto You
We lift our voice in praise

Unto You
Unto You
Unto You
Only You
We give our worship
All of our praise
Unto You

We give our love
Unto You
We give our strength
Unto You
We give our lives in worship

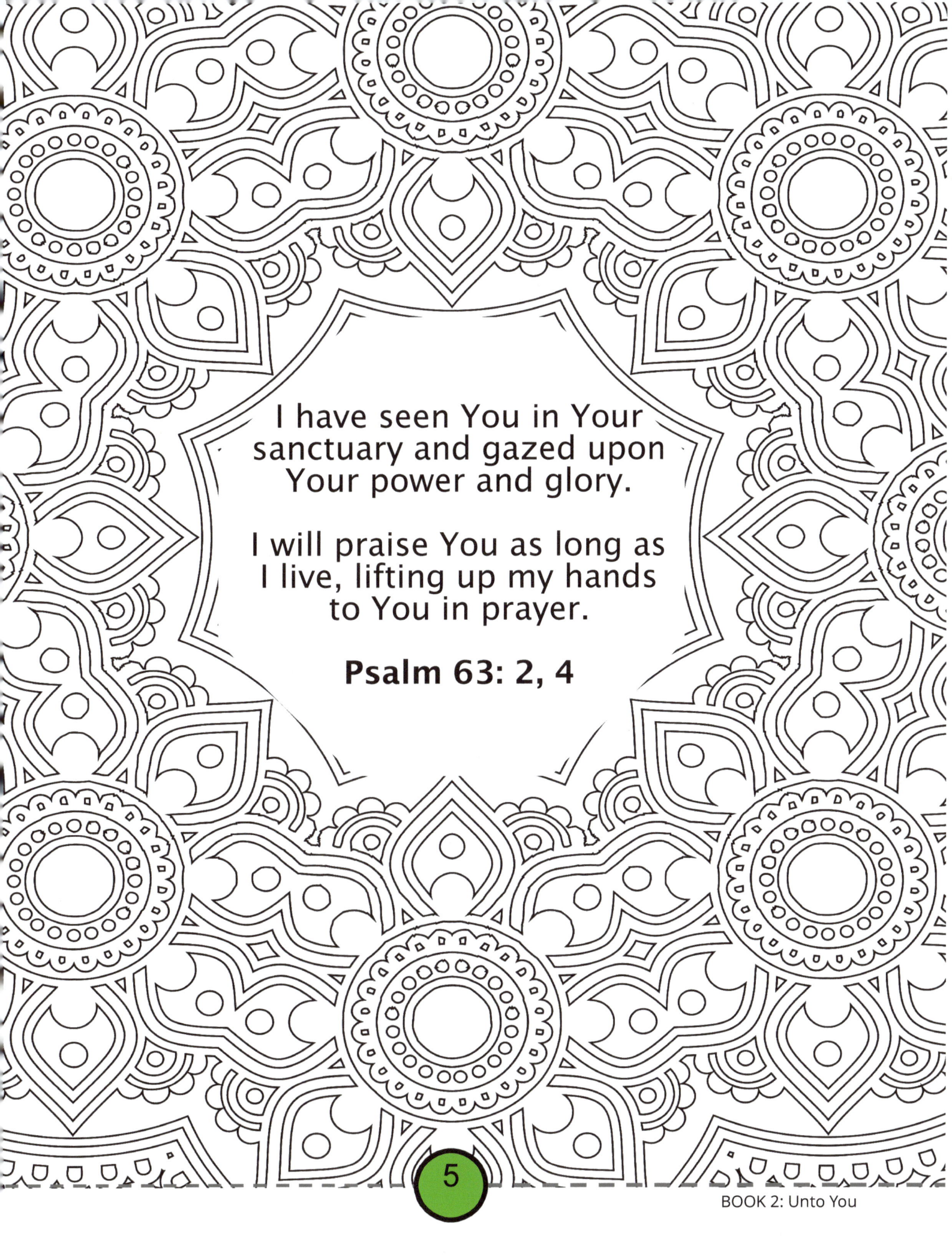

A CLOSER LOOK

We lift our eyes Unto You

When we sing **"We lift our eyes,"** we are not talking about looking up towards the ceiling or into the sky.

Lifting our eyes means focusing on God, instead of the things around us. As we look more closely at God, we discover more about who He is and what He likes.

When we 'lift our eyes' and see God, it helps us to understand who we have to be and what He wants us to do, so that we can please Him.

We lift our hands Unto You

A CLOSER LOOK

When **we lift our hands,** we are saying to God, "I surrender to You and give You everything. All I have is Yours."

Lifting our hands is an action we do on the outside that represents how we feel on the inside. It expresses what is in our hearts.

Psalm 63:4 reminds us that we lift up our hands when we praise God:

I will praise You as long as I live, and in Your name I will lift up my hands.

BOOK 2: Unto You

A CLOSER LOOK

We lift our voice in praise

When **we lift our voice in praise,** we are telling God that He is awesome and incredible - the best!

Lifting your voice means letting everyone hear the words that are coming out of your mouth.

So when it's time for worship, raise your voice and make a joyful sound to the Lord. Let God see how excited you are about worship. Don't be shy!

I will bless the Lord at all times; His praise shall continually be in my mouth. Psalm 34:1-3

Praising God with our voices together delights His heart.

Fill in the blanks with the missing words from the song.

We lift our _____
We lift our _____
We lift our _____ in praise.

BOOK 2: Unto You

We give our love - we always offer to God the best of what we have.

Giving love is an action we do, no matter how we feel. We give our love to God and to others through our thoughts, words and actions.

The Bible says, in **1 Corinthians 13:4-5**:

Love is patient. Love is kind. It does not want what belongs to others. It does not brag. It is not proud. It does not dishonor other people. It does not look out for its own interests. It does not easily become angry. It does not keep track of other people's wrongs.

Inside the heart, draw or write the things we offer to God.

You could talk to someone else about this for ideas and help.

**We give God everything:
All of our love, and all that we are.**

BOOK 2: Unto You

A CLOSER LOOK

We give our love Unto You

Do you remember the story of Cain and Abel? You can read about it in Genesis 4:3-7.

God was very happy with the offering Abel gave to Him, but unhappy with what Cain gave Him.

Abel gave the best of what he had **unto God.** We should always give our best to God; not just because our friends, teachers or parents tell us to, but because we want to please Him.

Use the number code to find the colors you need to color the picture below.

What do you see?

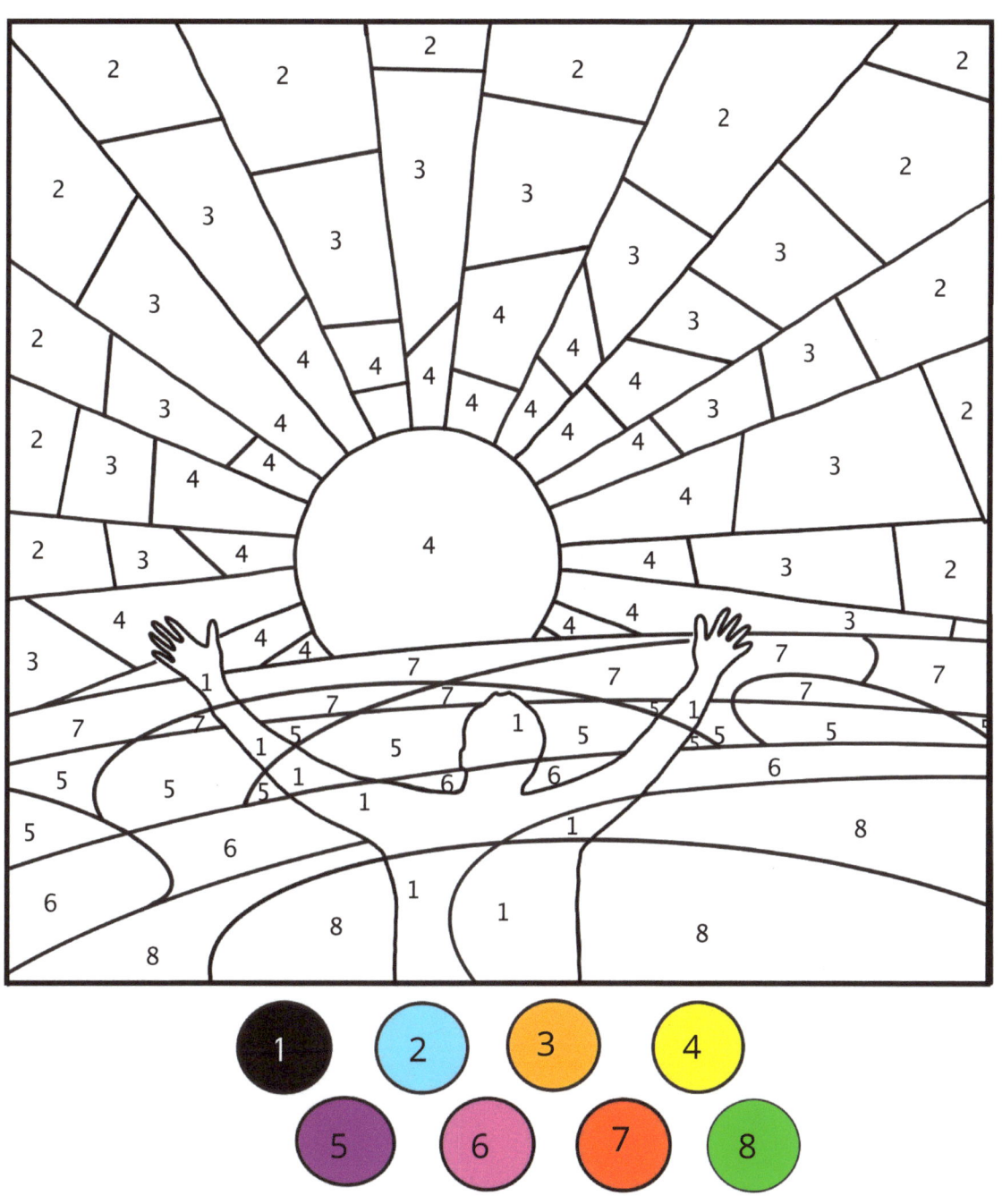

BOOK 2: Unto You

Think about when you had to use lots of effort and energy to do something. Maybe it was running a race, lifting something or studying for a test?

We thank God for the strength He has given us, and we offer it all back to Him when we worship.

We use the strength that we have in our body, mind, soul and spirit to give God our best, as we live for Him.

Deuteronomy 6:5: *Love the Lord your God with all your heart and with all your soul. Love Him with all your strength.*

Think about what it means to give God your strength. Draw a picture of you being strong!

BOOK 2: Unto You

A CLOSER LOOK

We give our lives in worship

The Bible talks about praising and worshipping God your whole life. This does not mean you walk around with your hands in the air singing all day long! But it does mean praising Him as long as we are alive.

We praise Him by our lifestyle. That means doing what pleases God, even when no-one is looking. For example, when we love one another, when we're honest, and when we obey our parents and leaders - this pleases God and gives Him honor.

Psalm 146:2
I will praise the Lord all my life; I will sing praise to my God as long as I live.

Unscramble the words, and then choose one of the words, and explain what it means to a friend.

| HIPSROW | ADHSN |
| _ _ _ _ _ _ _ | _ _ _ _ _ |

| IRPEAS | EESY |
| _ _ _ _ _ _ | _ _ _ _ |

| GTRHNTES | ECIVO |
| _ _ _ _ _ _ _ _ | _ _ _ _ _ |

ANSWER: WORSHIP, HANDS, PRAISE, EYES, STRENGTH, VOICE

BOOK 2: Unto You

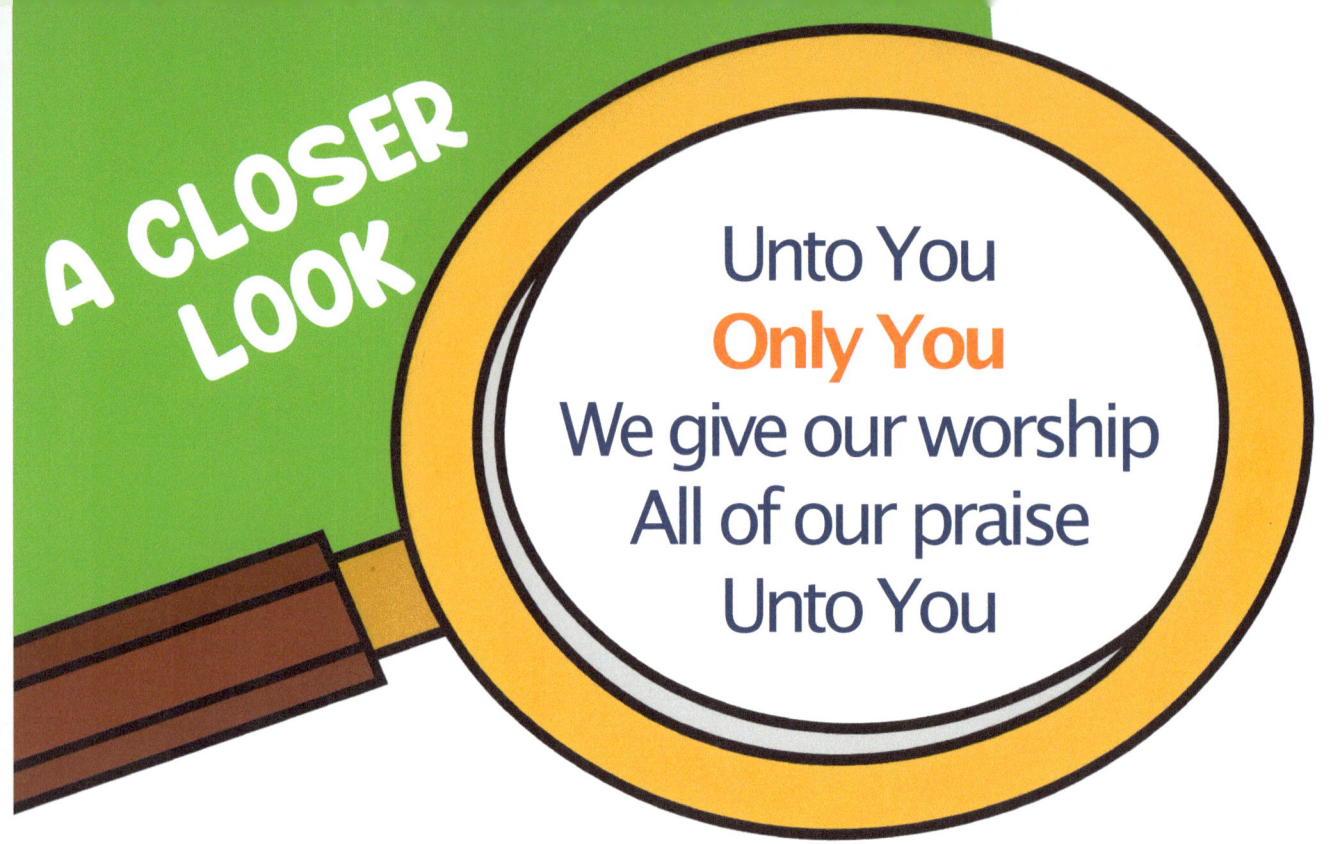

Only You means that we are willing to give up whatever we have, for God alone. These words are so simple, but very powerful.

When we say **"Only You,"** we focus all of our attention on God when it's time to pray, worship or study the Word. This means prioritizing God over other things in our lives.

We can enjoy playing with our toys and games, watching movies, playing sports or music—but these things will never have more value than the joy that comes from knowing God.

This song talks about giving our love in worship.

Write down some words in the hearts below that express your love for God.

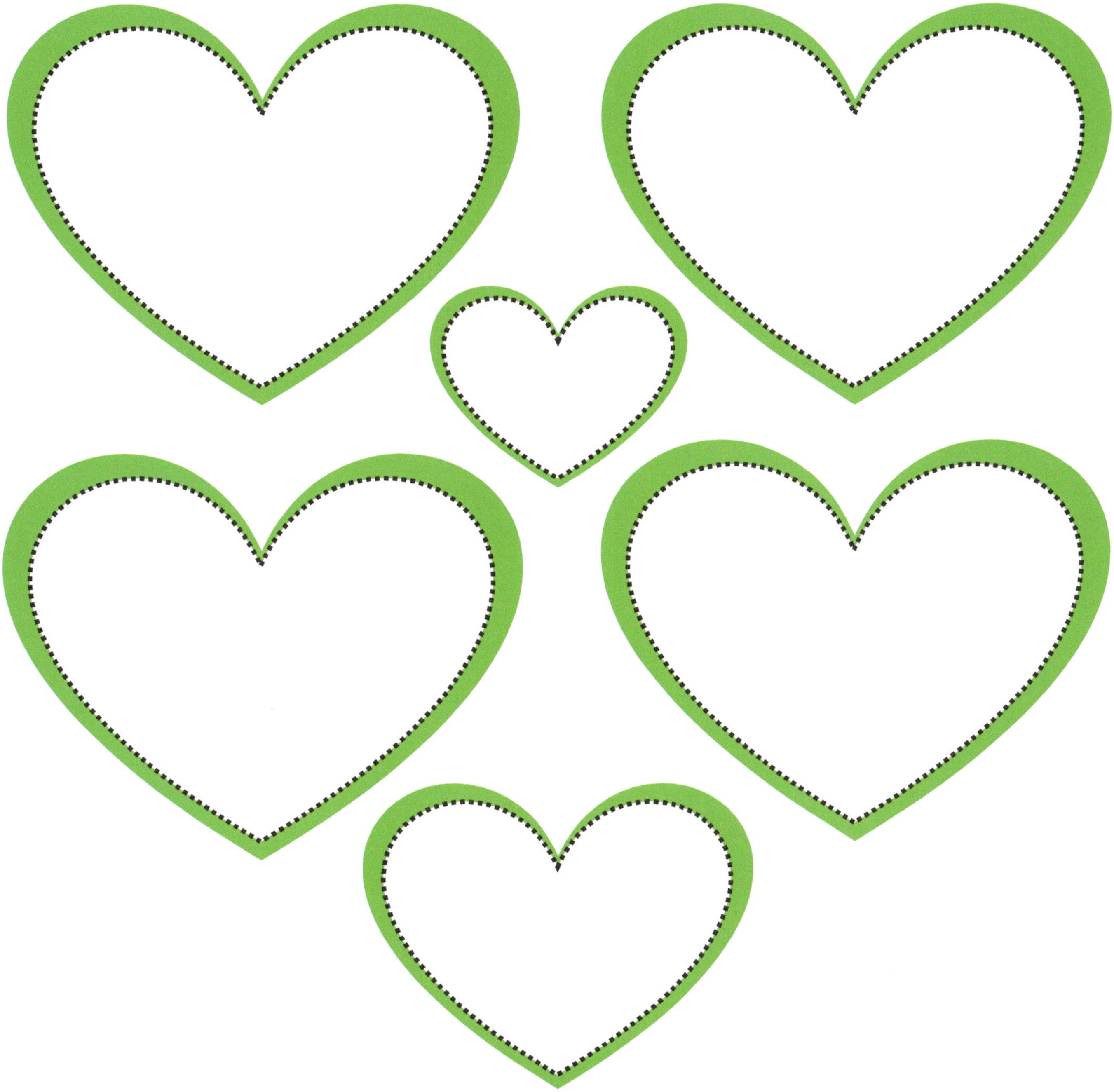

Take some time to reflect on this song. Here's some space to write down your thoughts.

MY JOURNAL

WE MAGNIFY YOU Discovery Workbook Series

www.ingramcontent.com/pod-product-compliance
Lightning Source LLC
Chambersburg PA
CBHW041123070526
44584CB00002B/258